Discovering RAILWAYANA

Donald J. Smith

Cover design by Robin Ollington

Shire Publications, Tring, Herts.

CONTENTS

The author wishes to acknowledge Messrs. Severn-Lamb Ltd., The National Trust, and staff of Penrhyn Castle Locomotive Museum, D. L. Gumbley, Esq., British Railways, The Severn Valley Railway Company, and The Welshpool and Llanfair Railway Company.

1. INTRODUCTION

Although railways have formed part of our civilisation for nearly a century and a half it is only in recent years that large numbers of people have taken more than a passing interest in their operation and development. There have always been railway enthusiasts, both amateur and professional, but these have greatly increased in numbers and depth of technical knowledge since the Second World War, especially during the past ten or twelve years.

By a strange paradox this new interest in railways lies parallel to their decline as a major form of public transport. It is only since the challenge of motorways, for both passenger and goods services, that preservation schemes have been launched, popular visits organised to railway installations and not even a remote branch line allowed to close without public ceremonies, television interviews and serious letters or articles appearing in the press. It is only during the second half of the twentieth century that trips have been arranged for railway enthusiasts taking them as far afield as South Africa, India, North America and Australia. More books are written on transport in general and railways in particular than on any other subject, while collecting and operating model railways has become one of the most popular indoor hobbies in the world.

At first the enthusiasm of a second 'railway mania' may seem little more than nostalgic and sentimental. The more advanced nations and cultures of the west have always tended to regret their past, especially during times of transition when there is a genuine danger of losing contact with former environment. Yet while to record and preserve something of the past may be described as either a duty or a luxury—according to outlook—it is seldom that such matters lie within the scope of ordinary individuals or those of average means. While historic buildings, valuable paintings and tapestries are the preserve of public bodies or persons of ample wealth, the collection of many items of railwayana lies open to the majority—from the schoolboy collecting tickets at pocket money prices to those wishing to acquire a locomotive, items of rolling stock, signalling equipment or even a complete railway station.

The future of railways and their economics are beyond the scope of these chapters. There are heartening signs, however, that modernisation and increased efficiency may win back custom from both roads and airways in the not too distant future. Promised schedules of 130 m.p.h. and upwards between the larger cities—centre to centre—may open the second great era of rail transport, no less exciting than the boom of the mid-nineteenth century. Yet it is keeping the railways efficient and up to the minute that helps to bring so many interesting relics before the public. Even British Railways have finally recognised the importance of railwayana and objects formerly scrapped or discarded are now preserved in transport museums or offered to the enthusiast at reasonable prices.

Historians are now increasingly aware of the importance of transport studies in understanding the development of civilisation. From this viewpoint alone a valid and not unattractive case may be made for the preservation of both railways and railway relics. Yet this is only one explanation of a complex subject. The need and interest to collect things of personal value lies beyond reasonable analysis. In the case of railwayana it is a mystery equalled only by the magic of railways themselves, finding devotees in all parts of the world. All that may be needed to start a collection are modest funds and storage space. Background knowledge may be acquired both in practice and by reading numerous books and magazine articles on railway subjects, to which it is hoped these lines make a useful contribution.

2. COLLECTING, CARE AND DISPLAY

As with most forms of collecting this aspect of railwayana needs both definite aims and careful selection. It is rarely possible, however, to be highly specialised in the early stages. Most people start with a piecemeal assortment, vaguely concerned with railways, lacking both coherence and more than personal interest. Yet as the enthusiasm grows there is also a tendency to cull out less valuable objects and search for items of particular significance. In this way the collector is eventually faced with a pattern of development clearly defined by objectives and limitations.

Many of the more obvious limitations concern the amount of money to be spent and space available for either storage or display. There are also limitations of size as locomotive nameplates and some of the larger items require a more spacious setting than a 'bed-sitter' or even the lounge of a small suburban house. It is ideal to have a converted garden shed, loft or unwanted garage space for the display of many larger objects—with the use of a work bench for cleaning and restoration purposes. Perhaps the most fortunate in this respect are those with the older type house—retaining a small stable block or range of outbuildings.

Items displayed in average-sized living-rooms are, of necessity, much smaller than those collected by enthusiasts for whom space is no object. In many cases they are of considerable interest from viewpoints of décor and ornament. Skilfully displayed items on a railway theme, including model railway equipment, have often proved ideal background material for club room, bar or restaurant, especially where fellow enthusiasts are likely to meet. It may be noted, however, that most items are heavy for their size and should be firmly secured to supporting base, background or wall surface.

Perhaps the majority of collections are of a general character, or at least commence in this form. Others may concentrate on such objects as lamps, block instruments, station signs or items of railway uniforms including braided caps, buttons, badges and armbands. Many enthusiasts restrict themselves to a particular railway company or region of British Railways. Others may limit their interests to light railways, overseas lines or relics of industrial and private systems. Whatever the angle of approach it is always an advantage to be well informed concerning the general background of railway history and technical knowledge. Useful contacts may be made with local railway officials and employees, who are frequently most helpful if approached with tact and consideration. The curators and officials of railway or transport museums are nearly always able to assist with problems of identification, while the Transport Records Office (B.R.) in London contains a wealth of evidence available to the general public. Certain public libraries in railway towns, such as Swindon, have complete sections of reference material ranging from makers' catalogues, handbooks and leaflets to Acts of Parliament.

Make a point of reading a general history of railways, with further study concerning the particular areas to which there is a bias of interest. While public libraries frequently have a transport section in their lending departments (other books being available on inter-library loan schemes) at least part of the collector's budget should be devoted to buying a few standard works. Supplement reading and theory with keen observation, travelling by rail as much as possible, and compare notes with fellow enthusiasts.

There are several ways in which railway relics may be acquired. Perhaps the most obvious is to buy direct from British Railways who now have a depôt for disposing of surplus and outdated equipment in Cardington Street, London—near their Euston terminus. A similar 'collector's corner' is also a feature of St. Enoch station, Glasgow, Carnforth (Steam Town) and several other stations. From time to time it is even possible to acquire surplus small items from the national transport museums at Clapham and York.

A number of railway bookshops have sprung to life during the past ten years, many of which also sell relics and souvenirs. Perhaps the best known of these—and a pioneer in the field—is the Roundhouse at Harrow-on-the-Hill. Some model shops also deal in the smaller items of equipment, especially those which concentrate on vintage models and quality items rather than on cheap plastic kits or toy trains.

Railway preservation societies and companies frequently assist their funds with open days, at which a popular feature may be a stall on which relics are displayed and offered for sale. Many societies have a permanent sales department which serves as a clearing house for smaller oddments, worth contacting when certain items may be needed to complete a set.

The magazines and periodicals devoted to railway interests usually carry several pages of small 'ads' devoted to the needs of collectors. These may be divided into trade advertisements and those concerning private sales and wants. While most relate to the sale or exchange of individual items many advertisers also issue price lists, in duplicated format, for which a small charge is made. A random selection from two classified pages of the *Railway Magazine* includes the following items: enamel signs, locomotive number plates, nameplates, bridge plates, lamps, tokens, trespass plates, tickets, timetables, whistles and carriage panel prints. These represent a fair cross-section of popular items, ranging in price from a few pence to upwards of £100.

One of the most exciting ways in which to acquire material for a collection is through the medium of public auctions. While a few of these are sometimes held in provincial towns (some organised and sponsored by British Railways) the majority are centred on London and are conducted by auctioneers with household names. Until about five years ago most of these concerns devoted themselves to the sale of 'old masters', first editions and antique furniture but, in view of popular demand, their interests have been widened to include railwayana, covering the range of items mentioned above as well as railway books and scale models. There are now at least five important sales each year in the West End conducted by such reputable firms as Christies, Knight Frank and Rutley, and Sothebys. Most auctions are advertised in the railway press while auctioneers are eager enough to supply catalogues and advance information. Viewing days are held just before the sale while those unable to attend an auction in person may arrange to bid through agents of the firm conducting the sale. The average sale of this type is a one-day event lasting from mid-morning until late afternoon, with a short break for lunch. As sale rooms tend to be fairly crowded it is advisable to arrive at least half an hour before time and claim a good position. No viewing is allowed on the day of sale.

While no societies are, as yet, organised for the sole purpose of collecting railway items, there are numerous clubs and groups—over a hundred in Britain alone—devoted to both general and particular railway interests. Joining one of these is fully recommended, as is a subscription to one or more of the excellent periodicals dealing with railways. Keeping in touch with outside events and market trends proves an important aspect of the hobby by any standards. Lists of selected periodicals and societies are given in Chapter 11.

Having acquired a number of items it is advisable to keep them in good condition, both improving their appearance and increasing their value. Many items from original sources have been imperfectly cleaned or totally neglected over a period of years and reach the collector covered with grease, rust or deposits of soot. It may be noted that, in this connection, a labour-saving device of the post-war era was to cover all bright work with layers of dark paint. Scraping off old paintwork to reveal unsuspected brass or copper mountings is one of the minor joys of restoration, especially with lamps.

Paintwork may also be removed from badly painted metal signs, or where it is thought necessary to restore an item to a pre-nationalised or pre-grouping livery. 'Polystrippa' is an excellent medium for this purpose and may be used on all surfaces and types of paintwork. See that all working parts, including catches and hinges, are thoroughly lubricated. Rust and tarnish are controlled through constant care—in such cases prevention being far better than cure.

The display of items is closely related to preservation. Some of the larger objects may be exhibited in gardens, safety valve covers and copper-capped smoke-stacks rising from the centre of flower beds wreathed in fronds of creeper.

Items exhibited indoors frequently look far better for mounting on polished boards or displayed under glass. If labels are necessary these should be kept as short and simple as possible, typed rather than written by hand—unless the collector is an expert at artistic lettering. In the latter case a neat round hand script is most effective.

3. LOCOMOTIVES AND STOCK RELICS

Nameplates

Perhaps the most obvious items in any collection are locomotive nameplates, being among the first relics brought to the notice of serious collectors.

The naming, as opposed to the mere numbering, of railway locomotives appears to have been favoured far more by some companies than by others. While certain railways limited this practice to larger tender engines designed for fast passenger services, others, especially smaller lines, were less discriminating and named most of their stud. Thus while the former Midland Railway almost ignored the idea, the Great Western gave impressive names to a large number of its stock, and the entire range owned by the London Tilbury and Southend Railway—apart from a few later engines—was named after London districts and suburbs. By a further paradox light railways, narrow-gauge branches and industrial systems, having some of the smallest locomotives in regular service, gave them highly romantic titles sadly out of place in colliery sidings, dockyards and gas works.

Naming locomotives, as with the later naming of trains, was often part of the brand image and brought useful publicity to a line in pre-grouping days, when there were so many parallel routes and rival services. Locomotives in the hands of the same crew for a number of years were often claimed to have developed a personality. The use of names seemed to encourage this cult, so that crews identified themselves more closely with their charges through added interest and efficiency. Even the most prosaic driver would feel more inclined to lavish care on *Lady of the Lake* or *Joyous Gard* than on a nameless saddle tank. Many, however, felt that names were only 'right' on large or important engines and it is significant that the Midland Railway, with its stock of nameless machines, was noted for small engines, having to rely far more on double-heading than other main line companies.

Nameplates are certainly a fine embellishment on an express locomotive, lending a touch of character even to less interesting machines. Plates were normally displayed as a pair and in a number of different places, depending on the type or class of locomotive. The position also dictated the shape and dimensions of the nameplate. The usual place was the crown or top of the splashers, which formed a protective casing above the top half of the driving wheels. This meant that the shape of the plate was curved to the arc of the splasher and might be long and narrow or short and squat according to the size of splasher—determined not only by the size of the wheel enclosed but also by the height of the running board above ground level. Thus a high running board frequently meant a shallow splasher and a restricted nameplate. Other nameplates would be oblong or rectangular, with either curved or square corners, fitted to boiler, smokebox, deflectors, running board or the face of the splashers. With the average run of steam engines the nameplate tended to be near the front end—corresponding on each side—although exceptions were made, as with locomotives of the LMS 'Coronation' class and streamlined 'Pacifics' on the Southern Railway. On some narrow-gauge and industrial locomotives, which are usually tank rather than tender engines, nameplates appear on water tanks or the side sheets of cabs. On broad-gauge engines of the GWR names appeared—either straight or arced—on the outer surfaces of sandwich frames, especially above the driving wheels of 'single wheelers' or those with 4-2-2 or 2-2-2 wheel arrangements.

While the majority of named engines are associated with the days of steam a number of more recent electric and diesel electric/hydraulic locomotives—both classes and individual engines—have also been named. These, however, often have smaller, less impressive plates than their predecessors, fitted in a central position on the sides of the upper bodywork.

In former days most named engines kept their original names and plates throughout their active lives, although a withdrawn or down-graded engine might pass its plates to a more efficient counterpart. A case in point concerns the above mentioned *Joyous Gard*—a 'King Arthur' class locomotive of the Southern Railway, which on being scrapped bequeathed its plates to a newly imported BR Standard Class '5' (No. 73088). Towards the end of steam on the main lines, many named engines were deprived of their nameplates long before reaching the scrap stage, as these had become targets for vandals and souvenir hunters. This tended to make the once proud flyer seem debased and neglected, although not perhaps as humbled as express engines on suburban duties or reduced to hauling a rake of assorted freight stock.

Most plates showed the name of the locomotive in raised individual letters, about an inch deep, cast in metal—frequently brass—and contrasted against a plain black or coloured ground. Some early plates, however, consisted of engraved or sunken letters on a raised background. The latter practice was followed by the LNWR, plates being made of brass without mouldings of any type. While some of these were curved others were straight, the latter appearing on the side of a composite splasher that enclosed not merely a single driving wheel but two or more wheels on the same side. GWR engines of the later 'County' class had similar oblong splashers, but name-plates—with raised letters—were displayed above rather than below or on the face of the splasher. The edges of most plates were surrounded by a moulding or beading of brass while, in some cases, spaces between the letters would be filled with black wax for the sake of greater contrast. Keeping name and number plates bright was a point of honour with engine crews of the 'old school'.

One of the most interesting features of nameplates concerns the great variety of designs in lettering and layout used by pre-grouping companies. There was, however, a tendency for lettering to be more austere and prosaic between the world wars. The Great Western was a remarkable exception in this sphere, retaining characteristic lettering right through to nationalisation, being the only survivor of the pre-grouping companies to retain identity unchanged by large scale amalgamations. A similar form of lettering has been adopted by the Western Region of BR—being successors to the old GWR—for nameplates on their diesel-hydraulic engines of both 'Warship' and 'Western' classes, although with shallower forms of raised letter than on steam classes. It may be noted that the GW style of lettering resembles a form of type face known in printer's idiom as Clarendon Bold (see plate 2). This was popular for monumental work, as well as for letter press printing, during the middle of the last century.

The secret of design in all plastic and graphic art lies in the correct balance between voids and solids. In the case of a locomotive nameplate this would refer to the way letters are arranged within the borders of the arced or rectangular base plate, seeming bold and impressive without overcrowding

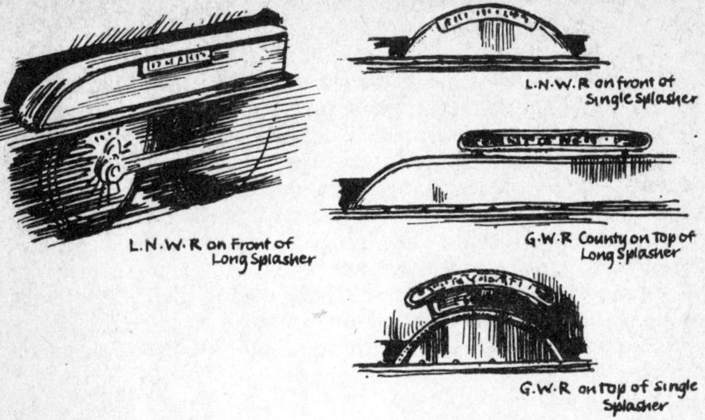

Positions of nameplates.

the background. Here again the Great Western frequently scored over its rivals, producing a nameplate remarkable not only for its style of lettering but also well spaced and easy to read. By contrast some of the lettering on Southern Railway and London Midland and Scottish nameplates tended to suffer from a feeling of tightness, with insufficient space between name and border, or between words—especially where several appear together as in *The East Lancashire Regiment* (LMS).

Lettering styles are either in simple block form—the bars of each letter being the same thickness throughout—or variations of the more graceful 'Roman' style with taperings or serifs finishing off the cross lines. Roman lettering also had the distinction of thick uprights and thin cross lines, diagonals being thicker when sloping from left to right than from right to left. Most lettering of the early periods tended to be elaborate but during the early 1930s the London and North Eastern Railway introduced a severe and economical style—shorn of all frills—designed by the sculptor and typographer Eric Gill. This was known as Gill Sans Serif and, at the time of its inception, was considered the last word in modernity. Although the individual forms seemed clean cut and chaste they lacked either strength or an intimate character and were mainly admired (by honest critics) for their beauty of layout or spacing. They formed a complete contrast with the more gracious forms preferred by the GWR and other companies, although appearing to greater advantage on the oblong plates of the 'A4s' rather than in semi-circular form on the shallow splashers of the 'V2' 2-6-2s.

Locomotives have been named after a wide variety of subjects and personalities ranging from crowned heads to classical heroes, racehorses and schools. The Great Western alone named their engines after cities, ladies, counties, courts, manors, halls, castles, kings, granges, saints, abbeys, stars, aircraft, flowers, birds and officials of their own company. The LMS introduced a wide range of regiments and corps of the British Army, nameplates surmounted by a military badge or crest. This tradition was revived during the 1950s when military titles and badges were appended to 'Peak' type '4' diesel electric locomotives with the 1Co-Co1 wheel arrangement.

'Hunt' class locomotives (4-4-0s) of the LNER were embellished with the replica of a running fox fixed to the top of each nameplate (see page 60). This appeared to be dashing along with brush extended as though chased by foxhound packs, such as *The Barham Moor* or *York and Ainsty,* after which the locomotives were named.

Bulleid-designed 'Pacific' engines of the 'Merchant Navy' class on the Southern Railway each bore a roundel with the house flag of a steamship company, surrounded by the name of the line concerned in circular form. Both the LNER and the Southern Railway named engines after famous schools, perhaps the best known of these being the SR locomotive *Eton.*

Although still appearing at public auctions or advertised through the medium of the railway press, locomotive nameplates are much harder to find than during the early days of the collecting mania. Apart from their decorative possibilities they are often considered a sound investment with prices soaring into hundreds for the more popular types. Some firms are now making either replicas of exact size or miniatures of the originals, charging so much per letter to the requirements of the customer (see plate 2). Foremost among these firms is Severn-Lamb Limited of Stratford-on-Avon, who were commissioned to replace nameplates on the preserved ex-WR locomotive *Burton Agnes Hall,* undergoing restoration at the Didcot depot of the Great Western Society. It is anticipated that these and similar replicas will one day become antiques in their own right. It has been further announced that a department of British Railways Workshops at Swindon will now supply aluminium name and number plates—among other items—although not in finished condition. Nameplates are similar to those appearing on the diesel-hydraulic 'Warship' class engines of the WR. They appear in cast condition but must be fettled and finished by the purchaser.

A small selection of nameplates recently viewed at the Cardington Street showrooms of British Railways (Euston), ranged in price from £180 to £50, including an unusual oblong plate from an early electric locomotive of the Metropolitan Railway, *Oliver Goldsmith,* at £75.

Although nameplates vary in size and shape even the smallest are by no means easy to handle or display. A large GWR plate may be nearly six feet across the base line. Those with limited space should restrict themselves to the smaller and lighter nameplates of industrial locomotives, narrow-gauge engines or replicas in such materials as aluminium.

Number plates

All locomotives are numbered irrespective of name or class. Number plates are of two main types, appearing either on cabsides or smokebox doors. The style or design of numbering usually harmonised with the style of lettering used by the same company, the GWR and WR providing some of the more outstanding examples. Cabside plates are larger than smokebox plates but less than half the size of locomotive nameplates. Being of a convenient rectangular shape they are much easier to handle and display than other large items. Some have been mounted on wrought iron legs and used as footstools or magazine tables. While smokebox plates fetch up to £20, cabside plates are usually worth double this amount.

Other plates of interest connected with locomotives include shed plates and works or builders plates. The typical shed plate is in the form of a small oval disc fitted to the lower part of the smokebox door at the front end of the locomotive. It merely records the shed code of the motive power department to which the locomotive in question is allocated, such as '2A' or '9B', in raised white letters on a plain background. These cost a few pounds each in the open market. Works plates are usually made of brass with raised letters and figures —sometimes on a red background—having the name of maker, town of origin, date of construction and serial number cast on an oval or rectangular base. The price of works plates depends on scarcity, many of the original manufacturing firms having ceased to trade during the past thirty years. A large number of British locomotives were produced in the workshops of BR or the former main line companies, and the Derby works of the former London Midland and Scottish (ex-MR) continued to turn out locomotives for BR with LMS plates for many years after nationalisation. A brass works plate in good condition, dating back before the grouping of 1922-23, may fetch up to £30 while later, less elaborate plates, are obviously much cheaper. Plates on electric and diesel multiple units and similar types of stock may be of thin brass or alloy, with shallow lettering, and sell for a pound or so each.

Tender capacity plates are oval or rectangular plates fitted to the rear of each tender, recording maximum water capacity.

Head boards, also known as train name boards, are either wood or metal, although usually the former, with raised letters of considerable depth made in one piece. When in use they are fixed to the upper bracket on the smokebox door of a steam locomotive or below the windscreen of a diesel or electric locomotive. They were originally made in a variety of shapes but are now mainly semi-circular, announcing either a named train or a special. Certain transport and other societies provide their own boards when embarking on a rail tour or excursion. The head board on the former named train *The Master Cutler* was made of stainless steel, in honour of the Sheffield craftsmen after whom it was named. The express linked London (Marylebone) with Sheffield over the former Great Central route.

Wagon plates

These are fixed to the underframes and solebars of rolling stock to record various details, including serial numbers and maker's name. As with shed and smokebox plates they are usually oval—but sometimes oblong—with raised block lettering on a plain background. Letters and numbers are usually white on black. The plate is framed within a raised edge or moulding.

Other small plates, with white lettering on a ground of black or navy blue enamel, gave details of private owners with instructions for repairs and handling in main line traffic (see plate 1). Many of the latter type were produced for the mineral wagons of collieries and coal merchants-factors before the Second World War and are now increasingly rare.

Carriage destination boards

These were long narrow boards usually fixed below the eaves or rainstrip of main line coaching stock. Those in good condition—hand painted—sell for a few pounds each. They were made of wood and coloured black on white or cream, white on red or a variety of colours to suit the company or region for which they were designed. Destination boards on the *Royal Scot* (Euston to Glasgow) had a tartan background. Each board measured up to a third of the carriage length and was fixed in a central position, held by a slot at each end.

Smaller name boards were sometimes fixed in brackets to the upper bodywork of a coach, either above or between the windows. Both long and short boards gave either 'to' and 'from' destinations such as London-Liverpool or the name of the express to which the vehicle was attached. In later years BR used square boards, with rounded corners, attached to the bodywork of coaches below the waistline. These recorded the destination and various stopping places.

Locomotive relics

While a limited number of funnels, domes and safety valve covers are still available, these are fairly expensive—in the same category as locomotive nameplates. Other smaller and slightly cheaper items from the footplate are in the form of taps, cocks, levers and gauges. Brass-mounted gauges are in fair demand, as are bell or organ type steam whistles, also in solid brass. Small lengths of hand-rail are sometimes available, complete with brass knobs, at reasonable prices.

Lamps

Large oil lamps are used on railways for a variety of purposes, those carried by hand, however, have now been replaced by more compact battery lamps. While either hanging or standard lamps are in fair demand the more popular examples include locomotive head lamps, lamps carried by guards and other employees, buffer lamps and lamps for level-crossing gates.

A typical GWR or WR three-aspect lamp, fully restored and in working order, would now be valued at about £5. Attractive copper-sheathed lamps, however, are worth more. Many early lamps have a prominent bullseye lens (see plate 3). While most lamps are square others are circular, both types painted either black or white. The cross handles are sometimes of brass but usually of steel, and the cap or knob over the filler is usually of brass, secured by a small brass safety chain.

Most of the larger lamps, including crossing and buffer lamps, fit into an outer casing, which opens at the top and clamps shut with a spring-type clip. Many buffer lamps have the front aspect surrounded by a plate or disc of 12 inches diameter. Both inner lamp and outer casing have cross handles.

Among the most impressive types of railway lamp are crossing gate lamps, about two feet high, mounted with copper and brass and painted red or black according to region. They are frequently four-aspect lamps filtered to show red at front and back and green at the sides. Each lamp is supported by a shank, bolted to the top rail of the gate by means of a steel clamp—the latter weighing about half as much as the lamp. These facts are mentioned to warn those intending to display a crossing lamp of the need to fix or mount the shank on a firm base. Unlike other lamps, which normally have a flat base, they are not always self-supporting.

In recent years there has been a limited demand for van and cart lamps, as used on horse-drawn vehicles and early motor lorries of the cartage services. These were still being produced for the main line railway companies up to the time of the Second World War.

It may be noted that locomotive head lamps were displayed on brackets fixed to buffer beam and smokebox door. GWR brackets were attached in a sideways position. Most sections of the main line system followed the rules of a simple head lamp code, so that it was possible to know the type and composition of a train from the position of the lamps. Rear lamps were fixed to the last coach of every passenger train.

4. STATION AND TRACK RELICS

Station name boards

A large number of the original name boards were scrapped shortly after nationalisation, long before collecting such items became either popular or profitable. In the days before the 1923 grouping each company had its characteristic signs, with flat or raised letters on either plain or coloured backgrounds. Raised letters were either cast in one piece with the background or individually screwed down to a flat base—being metal on wood. In both cases the name would be surrounded by a heavy moulding which might also serve as a protective rain strip. Southern Railway boards of the 1930s were frequently cast in concrete.

Some station name boards were quite large, including a whole list of other towns for which that particular stopping place might be the junction. A typical example was Craven Arms and Stokesay in Shropshire, originally served by two main line companies and having two separate boards on each platform. One recorded 'Craven Arms and Stokesay, Junction for Great Western route to Much Wenlock, Wellington and

Market Drayton'. The other board stated 'Junction for the Central Wales route to Llandrindod, Brecon, Swansea, Carmarthen, Tenby, Pembroke Dock and etc.'. Between them both boards were nearly as large as the side of a small house. Yet even these pale into insignificance beside the former LMS name board on Anglesey with fifty-eight letters—usually shortened to the first eight (Llanfair)—which claimed to be the longest place name in the British Isles. After the station closed, one of the boards was sent to the locomotive museum at Penrhyn Castle.

Another curiosity connected with station name boards was the polyglot sign appended to the board at Castle Bromwich near Birmingham, also on the LMS (now closed), formerly the headquarters of the heavy industries section of the British Industries Fair. This gave directions in four different languages for the benefit of overseas businessmen arriving by rail.

While most railway companies seemed to prefer simple, flat name boards between two upright posts, those on the Midland Railway were of double aspect fitted to a tripod. Lettering on most name boards and station signs was of block character and one thickness throughout, usually sans serif. The aim was to make them bold and prominent but as simple and legible as possible.

The older types frequently had raised letters although a few enamelled boards have been in existence for over fifty years. After nationalisation BR spent large sums on replacing existing name boards with enamelled signs in all parts of the country. These were in a variety of shapes and sizes but usually without mouldings. The smaller standard totems, as displayed on lamp-posts and walls, were in the form of a double oblong shape with rounded ends, the name appearing in the centre. Most of these, since the introduction of 'continental type signs', are also due for replacement.

Predominant colours for regional signs are white on maroon for London Midland Region, white on dark blue for Eastern Region, white on orange for North Eastern Region, white on light blue for Scottish Region, white on chocolate for Western Region and white on green for Southern Region.

Signal-box name boards

These are items which appear in greatly increased demand, especially since the introduction of modern forms of signalling and the rebuilding or closing of numerous boxes. They are either wood, cast iron or enamelled metal and range in price up to £15. The older boards with raised metal letters are usually more expensive, while enamelled signs are still fairly common in the cheaper range. It may be noted that most signal-box name boards were fitted in front of the box in a central position under the windows, although on some boxes they were slightly smaller and fixed over the door. The average length would be between ten and fifteen feet, although some of the smaller boards would be about four feet.

Door, direction and warning signs

A large variety of these are found in most station areas and at the lineside, being of cast iron with raised letters, enamelled metal or flat wooden boards with painted lettering. The usual colour schemes were the same as for station name boards, although large numbers were merely black on white. Signs for the Ladies' Room were sometimes white on pink in all regions.

Some of the larger signs were fixed directly to walls or fences while others were fixed at right angles to walls, posts or columns by means of brackets. Other signs—which resembled the arms of a country sign-post—were frequently mounted on a small platform reached by two or three steps with a guard rail, the whole surmounted by a clock face or dial adjusted to give the arrival time of the next train.

While most signs on platforms are intended to be read by passengers, others are for the instruction of train crews and other railway operatives. These may give warnings concerning the discharge of steam or ashes in a restricted station area or not to let locomotives stand on an over bridge. Boards found in goods yards prohibit locomotives from passing a certain point, usually the entrance to a covered goods shed with through road but limited head room.

Lineside notices and those outside station areas warn drivers to WHISTLE, SHUT OFF STEAM or BEWARE OF CATCH POINTS. Speed limits are shown by the number of miles per hour in Arabic numerals on vertical posts. Track repair signs are either a capital letter C (commence) on a round plate or a capital letter T (termination) on a square plate, both attached to a vertical post or upright. The sign for a water trough—from which locomotive water tanks and tenders may be refilled at speed, consists of an oblong board with four inverted V signs connected together at the base. Mile and quarter-mile posts appear at correct intervals, usually made of cast iron with black lettering on a white ground, distances measured from a zero post at the terminus of the main line. Gradient posts have two arms on opposite sides of a short wooden, metal or

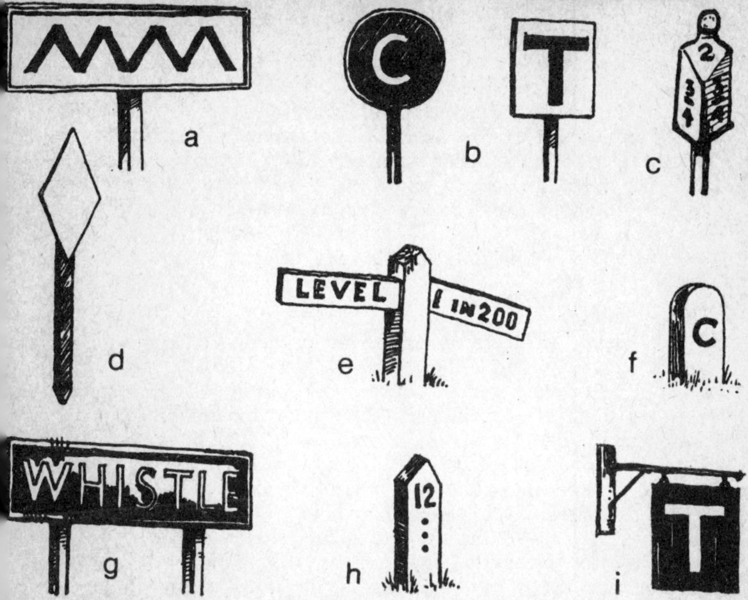

Track side signs: a, water trough sign; b, track repair signs; c, milepost; d, fog sign; e, gradient post; f, culvert post; g, whistle board; h, milepost; i, telegraph office.

concrete post, showing both gradient and level with each board inclined at the appropriate angle.

Whistle boards, trespass boards and the familiar sign BEWARE OF THE TRAINS are usually found in country districts, often near unmanned level-crossings. Trespass signs are also found on road or foot bridges over railways in all districts, frequently mounted on an unwanted length of rail. Many larger bridges taking a public road over a railway line may have a large diamond-shaped sign with raised letters, stating a list of size and weight restrictions for heavy vehicles and awkward loads. Similar boards are also found near canal bridges, many of the inland waterways being, for a number of years, controlled by main line railway companies. Round, square or oval bridge plates show the serial number of the bridge, frequently surmounted by the initials of the company for whom the bridge was constructed.

Fog signs are diamond-shaped plates on a post of medium

height. These latter are temporary signs denoting that fog signals have been laid on a certain stretch of track. A lineside drain or culvert is marked by a small white post with a rounded top, having a capital letter C in black on white.

Tokens for single-line working were frequently fitted with a looped end and attached to a vertical post near a junction with the main line, lit at night by a solitary oil lamp. The base of the staff fitted into a device for quick release set at an angle of 45° in the direction of oncoming trains—to be detached by a member of the crew leaning outwards from the driving cab.

Poster boards

These were a feature of many stations and halts of all sizes before nationalisation. They were also to be seen at the side of approach roads and sometimes on railway bridges. They were usually full or half sizes, also appearing as multiples of poster sizes. The average full sized board was 60 inches by 40 inches. The outer edge of the board was usually protected by a deep moulding while the name of the company—in either raised or painted letters—appeared in a separate panel of oblong shape above the advertisements. Lettering on boards of the North British Railway Company (Scotland) were noted for the rich shading and gilding of the hand painted letters. Replacement boards introduced by the LMS after the 1923 grouping were sometimes plain at the edges, without moulding or fluting.

Station furniture and external fittings

What might be termed portable exterior items include hand propelled vehicles, weighing machines and passenger seats or benches. Slot machines usually belonged to private vending companies, displayed on rented sites. The only coin operated machines other than lavatories, belonging directly to the railway companies, were platform ticket machines.

The most popular type of hand vehicle was the luggage truck with two small wheels, a ladder-shaped support and curved handles. The four-wheeled trolley or barrow frequently used for mail bags and larger items consigned by passenger train, frequently have brakes, which can be adjusted from handle or drawbar, the latter having either a loop or T-shaped hand grip. All platform vehicles were marked with load and tare weights in white lettering on a dark ground.

Weighing machines, apart from the elaborate personal weighing scales of Victorian origin, are usually found in goods yards, warehouses or luggage offices. They include a wide range of instruments from portable scales on small wheels to the parcels balance and counter platform scales.

Station or passenger seats and benches are of several company/regional styles in wood or metal, sometimes with a metal frame and wooden slats. The framework of some later seats was made from sections of pre-cast concrete. Nearly all seats have the name of the station or halt to which they are allocated, fixed to a plank of the back rest. Some, including both early and late designs of the Great Western Railway, have company initials interlaced either between the legs or forming a support in their own right. A number of these, introduced during the 1930s, included the ultra-modern roundel or 'shirt button' motif.

Hand tools

Locomotive shovels and firing tools, such as darts for raking clinker, etc., sell for a few pounds each. Småller items from the footplate include coal-pick heads, used for breaking up large lumps of steam coal.

Less frequently seen but still available in limited numbers are a variety of hammers used almost exclusively on railways or in railway workshops. These are used for wheel tapping, boiler making and scaling, rivetting and various platelayers' duties such as 'spiking' and 'keying' the track. Each of these have their distinctive character and appearance.

Other implements and hand tools in common use are mainly of interest to a collector when stamped with the name, initials or device of a particular company.

Furniture, china, cutlery and glass

Chairs and tables used in station offices or waiting-rooms, but sometimes from railway hotels and board rooms, are occasionally offered for sale. They are rarely expensive unless known to have been used by a figure of historic interest, or to date from the pioneer days of railways. Chairs of the type used by officials or station-masters, with high backs and armrests, may be sold in the region of £5 each, but only if stamped, carved or embossed with the crest-initials of a popular company. The importance of the label also applies to to a wide range of fairly common items from ticket dating machines (sold with boxes of type), filing cabinets and stapling machines. Fireplace fenders are also a popular buy, as are gas lamps of the suspended type.

Wall clocks, the earlier the better, if still in fair condition, make attractive ornaments, usually having the name or initials of the company on the centre of the dial. The official watches issued to guards, drivers and other employees now sell at about

£5 each. Those procured direct from British Railways, through their depôts and showrooms, are mainly in good order and require only cleaning and oiling before returning to active service. Watches granted for special conduct or long service are inscribed and far more expensive than those of standard issue. (Nearly all numbers on railway timepieces are in Roman rather than Arabic form. Those on older watches tend to fade.)

Crockery, cutlery and glass appear in an interesting and sometimes unusual range of designs. Since the recent nationalisation of the Pullman Car Company in Britain, large numbers of their spoons and forks have flooded into the market—usually of plated silver, although crests and initials may be worn down by long usage.

Leather straps of the type formerly used for raising compartment windows seem to be in demand at about £2 each. It is interesting to speculate how many were formerly purloined as razor strops, in the days before safety and electric razors. Even headrests of the antimacassar type, as used in first class carriages, find their market.

Pictures, framed and unframed, from both waiting-rooms and compartment interiors, sell in a wide range of prices. Those designed for compartments are mounted or matted in sets and known as carriage panel prints. Many of the pictures are reproductions of works commissioned from famous artists of the 1920s and 30s for publicity purposes. Many of these, however, suffer from the effects of damp or exposure and may be sun faded or disfigured by 'foxing' (brown damp stains).

Artists of the inter-war years producing better than average publicity material, with the accent on landscape and travel, include Tom Purvis, Frank Newbold, Austin Cooper, Fred Taylor and Gregory Brown. While Purvis, Newbold and Brown specialised in broad scenic views, Cooper and Taylor were more at home with architecture—especially the picturesque streets of cathedral cities and spa centres. Fred Taylor was frequently commissioned by the LNER and was in his element with a medieval setting. He produced a highly successful series illustrating alleys and byways of York, the finest of these being a view of Stonegate with busy shoppers wearing early Victorian costume.

Artists of international repute commissioned by the LMS included Sir William Orpen, the society portrait painter and war artist, who contributed a scene on the footplate of the *Night Mail*. Stanhope Forbes, a founder of the Newlyn School, better known for his Cornish landscapes, painted a typical scene of the old Midland Railway known as *Renewing the Track*. Norman Wilkinson contributed many fine pictures of harbour and coastal scenes, being an expert at shipping and seascapes.

Uniforms

Few of even the most dedicated collectors acquire what might be termed full uniforms. Most are content with caps, badges, buttons and armbands, of which there is a bewildering range and variety. Jackets and trousers of the old style, as issued before the 'Afrika Corps' uniforms of 1964, may be worth a few shillings or a few pounds each in the nature of WD surplus, of very little value from a collector's viewpoint. Greasetop hats of the type worn by footplate men in the days of steam are still fairly popular, as are caps worn by porters, foremen and other employees. Perhaps the most attractive and sought after item is the ex-GWR pillbox type cap of the 1900s, loaded with braid, which were still in daily use by senior officials after the Second World War. It may be noted that headgear and items of uniform are far more valuable if bearing the original badges, either braided, metal or woven.

A less familiar type of uniform relic appears in the form of stiff leggings or leather gaiters as worn by vanmen and goods agents until the 1950s. Numbers of these were recently available—in pairs—through Collector's Corner, selling for about a pound a pair.

Uniform buttons appear in three main sizes and were originally gilt, brass, chrome or white metal. Bone buttons of cheaper manufacture were introduced during the Second World War, partly as an economy and partly to save metal. Plastic types were available after nationalisation. All have raised crests or initial letters and make a highly effective display under glass. Buttons worn by station-masters, guards and senior officials were frequently of better finish and design than those worn by other grades and were stamped on the backs 'special quality'. Early buttons frequently show company initials in flowing script but changed to less elaborate styles shortly before the Second World War. Outstanding designs include the profile of a locomotive for the Taff Vale Railway, a mythical liver bird for the Mersey Railway, and three legs joined at the centre for the Isle of Man Railway. GWR designs (see plate 1) included both the joint arms of London and Bristol and different types of lettering. The GWR and the

LNER are known to have used about twenty-five different types of button.

Armbands, as worn by lookout men, may be further associated with the rattles, whistles, flags and warning horns worn or carried by such employees. Pilotmen, in charge of single-line working, wear green armbands. Badges and armbands are also worn by porters and railway employees working outside a station area.

Signals and signalling equipment

Early railway signalling was carried out by means of hand signals and the waving of flags. Early semaphore signals were frequently in the form of horizontal boards on low stands, discs and balls, all of which could be changed manually. More sophisticated signalling of the lower quadrant type was introduced during the 1840s but was not widely used until at least ten years later. Upper quadrants, a type of semaphore signalling in which the arm was raised rather than lowered (see plate 4) first appeared on the LMS during the 1930s.

The average semaphore signals of modern design may be mounted on a tall post or gantry and are used either as running signals for main lines or in sidings and goods yards. Junction signals are usually in pairs fixed to a narrow platform at the top of a single post. Running signals are either home or distant, the arm or board of the former being painted red with a vertical white band, while the latter are a bright yellow with a black chevron and inverted end or fantail. Both types have double glass spectacles with red/amber-green filters and a lamp fixed behind the spectacle in position.

The tops of most signal posts have an ornamental capping or pointed finial, some being several feet tall and making splendid garden ornaments. A typical GW finial now sells in the region of £5.

Signal arms are either wood or metal, the earlier or lower quadrant type taking the form of a plain wooden board—while upper quadrants were metal plates with horizontal grooves or rainstrips. Special signal boards used to control the entry to goods yards had a white ring at the end of the board furthest from the post. What were known as shunting signals had a capital letter S in a similar position. Both the latter types were lower quadrant, operated at horizontal for danger and lowered for all clear.

Smaller varieties of shunting signals appeared either in the form of discs near ground level or miniature semaphore types.

Various items of equipment from signal-boxes include repeaters, indicators and block instruments, some of which

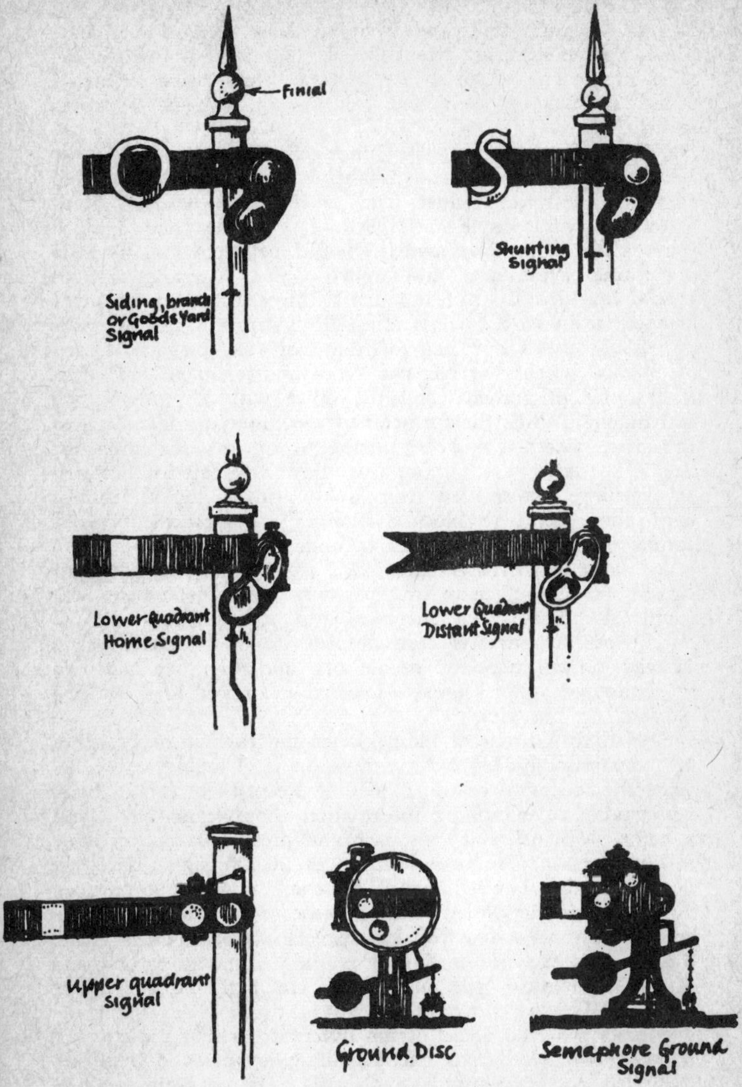

Different types of signal.

are still available from pre-grouping days. They make handsome ornaments, being about the size of a large drawing-room clock of the late Victorian era, mounted in a casing of highly polished wood. A combined bell and instrument is worth about £15.

The following brief notes may serve as a guide to the functioning of signal-box equipment, of the types mentioned above. The most popular item is the three-position block instrument and single-stroke bell. The former had a clock face or dial with three panels divided between 'line blocked' or 'normal', 'line clear' and 'train on line'. A single hand or needle in the centre of the dial is pivoted to one or other of these sections. A later type of BR instrument had all three panels on the lower half of the dial (see plate 5). Each mechanical signal-box has two types of instrument, one with a 'pegging instrument' and the other with a 'non-pegging instrument'. While the former had a commutator handle near the base, which could be turned to operate the indicator needle, the latter was without a handle and repeated indications or warnings transmitted from a box further up the line—controlling the next block section. These instruments were connected by overhead wires or underground cables.

On some of the older main lines, especially in the Southern Region, a less efficient two position block instrument was frequently used. This survived into the post-war era of nationalisation but has been obsolete now for several years. Instead of an indicator needle or hand the dial had two miniature semaphore signals—lowered and raised to show 'line blocked' or 'line clear'.

Signalling was one of the neglected but fascinating branches of the railway hobby, but the position is changing, especially since the inception of the Signalling Record Society in 1969, which aims at compiling information about signal-boxes and systems of British Railways, past and present. It is incredible to think that there were once over 20,000 signal-boxes in Great Britain alone, Many of these are now being replaced by the introduction of multiple-aspect or robot signalling controlled from a few panel boxes placed many miles apart. This means the closing and demolition of many early boxes of the mechanical type, of which there might be no further trace but for the efforts of the S.R.S.

Members of the Society from different parts of the country make drawings of track and signalling layouts and these are compiled and exchanged. Such efforts range from a small branch-line box drawn on a sheet of foolscap, to a diagram of the ex-GWR box at Bristol East, which contained 368 levers, and occupies an area of tracing paper seven feet in length. The Society is also engaged in building up a collection of photographs of signal-boxes and their fittings on a national scale, with details of openings, closures and alterations. Individual members collect a wide range of items from block instruments to train staffs and tokens used in single-line working. The Society archivist has information on about 5,000 signal-boxes, of great value to historians, writers and students of transport history. Bi-monthly newsletters are circulated and visits arranged to installations in all parts of the British Isles. Membership is open to all of sixteen years or over, on application to the Secretary (see Chapter 11).

5. TICKETS, TIMETABLES, ETC.

Tickets

These have been collected by boys of all ages as long as stamps and much longer than cigarette or trade cards. They may be displayed under glass or in loose-leaf albums similar to those sold to philatelists, although stamp hinges frequently cause damage (and subsequent loss of value) to one side of the ticket in question.

The value of tickets to the ordinary collector may vary from pounds to pence, rare specimens from closed systems or defunct branch lines fetching comparatively high prices for partly nostalgic and sentimental reasons. Those of the better known Irish Railways and such lines as the Liverpool Overhead Railway may be bought for ½p each. While various types and qualities of ticket have been issued from thin paper to stiff card, including semi-stiff or semi-card—the latter frequently used on light railways—the most durable and effective are the Edmondson card tickets printed by letter press. The standard type of Edmondson ticket is now used in all parts of the world, dimensions being 1 3/16 x 2¼ x 1/32 inches. They were invented by Thomas Edmondson, a booking clerk on the Newcastle and Carlisle Railway in 1837. Earlier tickets were written by hand with a duplicated counterfoil.

Tickets are issued for a number of special purposes including single or return fare, excursions and half-day excursions, with special tickets for schoolchildren, workmen, forces on leave, cycles, dogs and prams. Other tickets are issued for admittance to platforms, as certain closed stations cannot be entered without showing a ticket or pass of some description. Platform tickets cost from ½p to 1½p, and may be purchased from a special slot-machine near the barrier or from the ticket window. At certain stations of the former LNER, in the eastern counties, free platform tickets could be obtained.

Since the 'Beeching axe', with wholesale closure of branch lines and country stations, large stocks of unused tickets (withdrawn) are now available in bulk. Many of these still bear the name or initials of former main line companies of the post-grouping era. Whole tickets are worth far more than halves, while those in good condition are preferred to dirty or damaged specimens.

Those wishing to specialise in the collection of railway tickets should contact the Transport Ticket Society, which circulates a regular news-sheet in which both collections and individual tickets are offered for sale or exchange (see Chapter 11).

Stamps and railway letters

Stamps showing pictures of locomotives or views of general interest to railway enthusiasts are now widely collected, forming a special branch of philately. Their subjects are far more varied and interesting than the novice might expect, having been issued by countries in six continents—even by those such as the republic of San Marino without railways of their own. Perhaps the most prolific countries in this respect are Belgium, the countries of Eastern Europe, and the republics of South America. It has been estimated that over 1,000 railway subjects have been printed in seventy countries.

Many of the stamps show famous locomotives, both ancient and modern, being mainly commemorative or to record the opening of a new station, bridge or section of line. East German issues recorded the 125th Anniversary of German Railways, while a United States postage stamp 'Honouring Railroad Engineers of America' paid tribute to the self-sacrifice and heroism of the legendary Casey Jones. Other US stamps celebrated the 125th Anniversary of the Baltimore and Ohio Railroad Charter, granted in 1857, and the opening of the first American Trans-continental System in 1869.

Some of the latest and most interesting recent stamps were issued by the government of Jamaica on November 25th 1970, to commemorate the 125th Anniversary of the Jamaica Railway Corporation, with values of 3, 15 and 50 cents. The lowest value shows the *Projector,* a 2-2-2 tender engine of 1845; the 15 cent stamp is of a modern steam type now ear-marked for preservation; the highest value shows an 'Alco' diesel-electric engine (No. 102).

In Great Britain, the home of railways, the GPO (up to 1971), have not issued postage stamps showing railway items or locomotives. In 1964, however, the northern railway town of Stockton-on-Tees, associated with the first passenger line constructed by George Stephenson, issued a local postmark with a profile of the famous Stephenson engine *Locomotion No. 1*.

Three privately owned British systems have also issued special stamps with railway views, for use on railway letters. For many years after nationalisation, however, the Talyllyn narrow-gauge line in North Wales was the only private concern to issue railway letters (see plate 6), but in 1969 the Festiniog Railway and the Ravenglass and Eskdale Railway followed suit.

The first British railway letters were issued in 1891 as the result of an agreement between the GPO and certain independent railway companies. The main purpose was to ensure a speedier service for individual letters—at a slightly higher charge—similar to first class mail. Nationalised BR continued to make use of this service, issuing a parcel type label in place of the special stamp required in addition to ordinary postage dues. Special railway stamps have also been issued for use on the Vale of Rheidol branch, the only steam operated (narrow-gauge) branch line of BR after the official passing of steam in 1968.

Railway letters are often distinguished by elaborate pictorial covers, especially those issued by narrow-gauge and preserved lines

Books and leaflets

These are always of interest to the serious collector, either for their own sake or as a guide to further knowledge. Most railway books in good condition are a worthwhile speculation continuing to appreciate in value, both in and out of print. For the most part they fall into two main categories—those of an official character written for and by railway officials and those about railways aimed at either the serious student or the novice.

Apart from the personal pleasure to be gained from collecting railway books and documents it should be remembered that anyone building up a special library over a number of years may be rendering a service to future generations, especially if arrangements have been made for it to be cared for and disposed of in quarters where the books may be most appreciated. It is also possible to realise fair sums on such a library, through the medium of a London or provincial railway auction, many of which have sections devoted to books, bound magazines, leaflets and other printed matter connected with railways.

Timetables (both public and working), shareholders' and travel guides (both the latter published by Bradshaw), handbooks on particular railway systems—sometimes produced by the company concerned—are all useful acquisitions. Bradshaw's guides are now, however, very rare and much sought after at prices well beyond the range of average collectors. Many early guides and timetables were unfortunately destroyed in the paper drives and salvage schemes of the Second World War, at a time when their value was scarcely worth the paper on which they were printed. Even the colourful holiday guides such as *Holiday Haunts,* published between the world wars by the main line companies, are now prized by certain enthusiasts.

Those who wish to have a more than superficial knowledge of the inner workings of railways should make a point of acquiring not only working timetables but also the various rule books and operating instructions published by individual companies and regions of BR.

These deal with every likely and many unlikely subjects from 'painting vacuum train brakes' to 'watering livestock in transit' and 'collection of tickets from military escorts or persons in charge of special machinery'.

Other sources of information are the railway year books, still published on an annual basis but now entitled the *Directory of Railway Officials and Year Book.* Back numbers of these recorded not only the assets and ramifications of a railway company but also served as a guide to all grades of officials, engineers and executives who helped to expand the international system and keep it in working order.

Trade catalogues, leaflets and brochures produced by some of the leading manufacturerers of locomotives and railway equipment, such as Robert Hudson, Thos. Ward, Hudswell, Clarke and Peckett of Bristol are nearly always worth acquiring at reasonable prices—below the £5 margin.

Another useful buy for the serious student and enthusiast is the official *Hand Book of Railway Stations,* published by the Railway Clearing House until the Second World War. This gives information concerning every station, halt and siding in the United Kingdom, noting all connections from private concerns such as factories, quarries and mines—with details of crane power and facilities for handling livestock, parcels and many allied problems.

In collecting magazines and journals of railway interest it is advisable to have these bound—as soon as possible—in stiff covers. Without such precautions they soon fall to pieces. Most firms publishing railway magazines undertake to bind their annual offerings—complete with index—in sturdy cases, at realistic prices. With bound magazines it is nearly always easier to trace an elusive article than by flipping through numerous loose covers.

6. MODEL RAILWAYS

The model railway hobby has undergone an unexpected renaissance during the past decade, and now includes large numbers of people who not only operate and construct their own layouts, but who collect both toy trains and elaborate scale models.

While 'scratch building' and operating are enjoyable in their own right it is mainly the collecting side of the pastime that concerns the reader of these chapters. To the average enthusiast scale models are sure to have an obvious appeal, forming an extension to the collection of lamps, nameplates and other items in the round. A finely modelled locomotive in a glass case is an enviable acquisition in any household and, judging by recent trends, may soon challenge the model galleon or clipper as an accepted item of decorative interest.

While many people would be able to appreciate the craftsmanship and decorative appeal of a scale model it is perhaps less easy to define an enthusiasm for old tinplate engines and railway accessories. With many collectors of model railways and toy trains buying a few odds and ends is frequently the prelude to operations. While a model locomotive is charming enough on the shelf even the least curious may feel an urge to see the motions work and the wheels go round. Models intended for work are usually of greater value if advertised in working order, which naturally leads to a simple test track on a portable baseboard, leading—in the course of time—to a permanent branch line in the loft or an experimental layout through the rock garden.

Model railways are certainly an interesting hobby, by any standards, involving a wide range of artistic, craft and mechanical skills. Their varied scales and gauges range from the near microscopic to passenger-carrying equipment more correctly termed miniature railways. The first models produced on a commercial scale were mainly imported into Britain from Germany during the second half of the nineteenth century. They were stocked, during the early winter months, in the unlikely windows of chemists and haberdashers, and were given to mechanically minded boys as Christmas presents. W. J. Bassett-Lowke, formerly the doyen of British model railways, was apprenticed to the family engineering works in Northampton during the 1890s, but was already making a profitable sideline out of scale fittings and components for the increasing number of serious modellers. After visiting a continental trade exhibition and making contacts with several foreign manufacturers he decided to develop the potential of the home market by making and selling a complete railway system designed by himself or his assistants from authentic British prototypes. Bassett-Lowke models became a household name and were familiar in thousands of British homes for over fifty years. While selling a number of excellent models—made to the highest possible standards—the most typical Bassett-Lowke products were in the medium price range offering character and performance allied to strength and durability. Compared with both earlier and later models, either functioning correctly but looking atrocious or performing badly while appearing immaculate, Bassett-Lowke offered not so much a compromise but a solution. The Northampton firm and its offshoots were also pioneers of passenger-carrying scale models, or miniature railways, of the type frequently seen in pleasure parks or at seaside resorts. These were not only designed and manufactured at Northampton but frequently operated by the parent firm, Mr. W. J. Bassett-Lowke taking a keen personal interest in this side of the business. Even before the First World War there were Bassett-Lowke designed or inspired miniature railways at Rhyl, Southport, Blackpool, Halifax, Sutton Park (Sutton Coldfield, near Birmingham) and Fairbourne (North Wales). Several similar lines were also laid in the private parks and gardens of wealthy patrons (see plate 7), and became a regular feature of the great national and international exhibitions of the period.

The commercial challenge was further taken up, after the First World War, by Frank Hornby, inventor of the construction toy 'Meccano'. Although thoroughly reliable and strong the majority of Hornby models, however, appealed more to younger boys than to the older or better informed enthusiast. While they could be dropped from a bedroom window without serious damage they were seldom based on real engines or prototype equipment—until the late 1930s,

K. Bennett

1. *Railway relics, including a private-owner wagon plate, WR and ex-GWR buttons, and a spike from a North Wales Quarry Railway.*

Severn-Lamb Ltd.

2. *Replicas of GWR nameplates, made by Severn-Lamb Ltd.*

3. *Crossing and buffer lamps.*

K. Bennett

M. Williams

4. *A typical main-line country station on the former MR, Water Orton, showing the BR name board and the upper quadrant signals.*

D. L. Gumbley

5. *A block instrument used in railway signalling (from the collection of D. L. Gumbley, Esq.).*

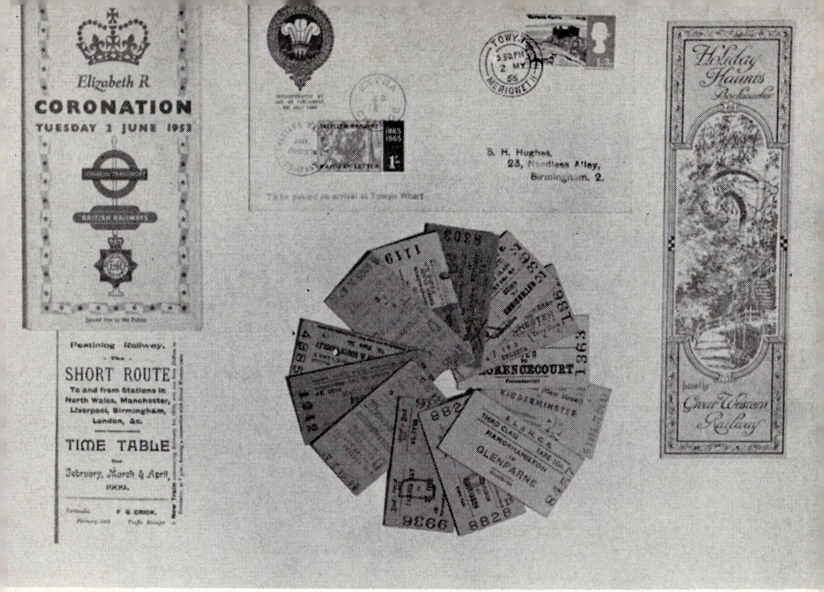

K. Bennett

6. *Railway relics, including tickets and a railway letter from the Talyllyn Railway.*

7. *W. J. Bassett-Lowke driving a $4\frac{3}{4}''$ gauge model engine on a railway constructed by his firm for the late Sir Berkeley Sheffield.* W. J. Bassett-Lowke & Co. Ltd.

D. L. Gumbley

8. *'Earl of Merioneth', a Fairlie Patent locomotive on the Festiniog Narrow Gauge Railway.*

9. *Open day at the Severn Valley Railway.*

D. L. Gumbley

D. L. Gumbley

10. Courtauld's locomotive shed on the Foleshill Railway in 1969 with a large Peckett (1948) standing outside.

11. Part of the 'Midland Railway' layout at Derby Museum.
Derby Museum

David E. Sutcliffe

12. *An ex-LNWR 'coal tank' arriving at the Penrhyn Castle Locomotive Museum (by kind permission of The National Trust).*

when a belated attempt was made to introduce a few scale models that might 'rub shoulders' in better company. As with Bassett-Lowke railways the Hornby firm offered a wide range of rolling stock and accessories including signals, stations, viaducts, water towers and lineside advertisement hoardings. The equally famous 'Dinky Toys' were first developed to supplement the Hornby layout with miniature figures, road vehicles and farm animals—dummy hedges, trees and bushes being available to divide lineside areas into roads and fields.

Other firms eventually sharing the competition (of which only a few survived the Second World War) produced model railways with either great attention to detail or as mere travesties—mainly according to price range and sophistication. Several firms, including Edward Exley (renowned for scale model rolling stock), made not only commercial models to sell over the counter but scale models in the exhibition class, to order. Bonds, the Leeds Model Company, Hamblings and Mills Brothers were all names to conjure with during the 1920s and 1930s. Fortunately Bonds, Hamblings and Exley are still with us although in slightly different circumstances from their predecessors. The activities of Bassett-Lowke are now represented by the Steam Age shop in Chelsea, while Hamblings are still a great depôt and clearing house for the smaller gauges. The Exley firm have been making scale models for both private collectors and exhibitions—in company with Bassett-Lowke—right up to the 1970s.

During the 1930s scales and gauges tended to get much smaller, to suit the trend towards smaller houses and flats. This policy continued when production revived after the Second World War. General standards also improved, with a greater demand for realism in the cheaper ranges. While the best of the old models are often without equal the popular ranges are now much better than ever before.

Few model railway collectors are above making slight adjustments in the cause of up-grading their stock, although the majority agree—on the subject of paintwork—to leave well alone. The original and authentic livery, despite a few scratches and bruises, is half the charm of an early model, especially those in the tinplate range.

An effort should be made, wherever possible, to retain the original box, packing materials and instructions, all of which add to the period charm. Even models needed for static display only are better for an occasional run and should be kept oiled and serviced with this in view. Do not over-oil electric models. Make sure that all models, working or otherwise, are protected by a warm, dry, but not too dry, atmosphere.

Catalogues of model railways are now quoted in sale rooms and through the press, at almost unbelievable prices, and have boomed almost as much as the models they advertise. Those from the pre-1914 era are among the most valuable with any leaflets or catalogues bearing the Bassett-Lowke imprint in great demand. Hornby train catalogues are also popular in a slightly lower price range and are now being reprinted for the sake of Hornby fans, originals being in short supply. Large numbers of British, European and American catalogues are produced annually, with an exceptionally high standard of colour printing and layout, not forgetting some worthy contributions from Japanese manufacturers—since the late 1950s. Some of the finest British examples of the last ten years have been published by the firm of British Trix, originally a small-gauge off-shoot of the Bassett-Lowke concern. While forming a source of information and reference material for the average collector, the catalogues of today are the treasures of the future, worthy of a corner of the collector's bookshelf rather than the dustbin or incinerator.

7. PRESERVED LINES AND INDUSTRIAL RAILWAYS

These have a particular interest for the enthusiast who likes to feel part of an organisation, playing an active role in keeping alive not only working exhibits but the authentic atmosphere of the steam age. There is now a wide range of preserved branch lines, both narrow and standard gauge, needing the active work and financial support of new members. By joining one of these groups, many of which are now formed into limited companies for the purpose of obtaining a light railway order, there may be opportunities to learn and practice the skills of driver, signalman, guard or shunter on a week-end summer holiday basis. An even wider range of semi-skilled or unskilled jobs from track maintenance work to running a bookstall are available for the less adventurous.

Modern railway preservation, as opposed to collecting relics and saving the odd engine from the scrap merchant, began with the Talyllyn scheme based on the Wharf station at Towyn in North Wales, which is also the site of an interesting narrow-gauge museum. The **Talyllyn Railway** of 2′ 3″ gauge, first opened in 1865 to serve the slate quarries of Bryn Eglwys, but later ran both goods and passenger services over about twelve miles of track. Although closed in 1951 as a direct result of road competition and the closure of the slate workings, the line was revived by a band of enthusiasts and became the first system of its kind to be saved from destruction.

Perhaps the most picturesque and spectacular of the preserved narrow-gauge lines is the 1′ 11″ gauge **Festiniog Railway** (plate 8). This has 9½ miles of track winding through superb mountain scenery on the borders of Merioneth and Caernarvonshire in North Wales. It began life as a quarry railway in 1836, the first sections being operated by gravity and horse haulage. Locomotives came to the line in 1863, followed two years later by regular passenger services. Closed in 1939, as a result of wartime conditions, it was later purchased by Mr. A. F. Pegler (owner of the *Flying Scotsman*), who reopened the line as a tourist attraction in co-operation with a flourishing preservation society. One of the main attractions, from the viewpoint of railway enthusiasts, is the varied range of motive power including a 'Garratt' engine from Tasmania and two 0-4-4-0 Fairlie Patent locomotives with back to back profiles.

The **Welshpool and Llanfair Railway** is one of the few remaining systems of the once popular 2′ 6″ gauge remaining in working order. This is also the domain of enthusiasts and part-time railwaymen, mainly from the industrial areas of the Midlands. Formerly operating between the market town of Welshpool and the even smaller town of Llanfair Caereinion, to serve local agricultural and forestry interests, it is now reduced to about 4½ miles of track between the latter centre and Castle Caereinion, with the prospect of extensions to a new terminus at Welshpool when funds become available. The scenery through which it runs is typical of the northern marches or border counties of Wales, being pastoral rather than rugged or wild. Present stock includes the two original locomotives built in 1902 and an assortment of both British and continental rolling stock, a number of passenger coaches having been obtained from a similar preserved system in Austria, with which there are fraternal links.

Other interesting narrow-gauge systems are operated in the **Isle of Man, Bicton Gardens,** East Budleigh, **Cadeby Rectory** (Leicestershire) and at **Bressingham Hall** (Norfolk).

Standard-gauge preservation schemes range from a few hundred yards of track in an abandoned motive power department to complete branch lines. What might be termed the senior of these undertakings is the **Middleton Railway**

Trust, which operates a three mile section of track between a junction with British Railways and privately owned factory sidings. Its route covers the remaining part of the first railway in Britain to receive an Act of Parliament (1758) and the first railway to convert from animal haulage to steam power. It is now protected by the National Trust, but is very much a working railway, handling genuine goods traffic throughout most of the year. Passenger trains are run on various open days.

Several schemes aimed directly at the tourist and holiday-maker combine the pleasures of a day out with the more specialised and technical side of railway preservation. These include **The Keighley and Worth Valley Light Railway** (Yorkshire), **The Bluebell Railway** (Sussex), **The Dart Valley Railway** (Devonshire) and **The Severn Valley Railway** (Shropshire). All of these operate as pleasure lines and may also be termed working museums. Both Dart Valley and Severn Valley lines have a distinctly Great Western bias—being in the heart of former GW territory—although the Severn Valley (plate 9) also owns a certain number of carriages and locomotives from the Midland Region, redolent of the former London Midland and Scottish Railway, which sometimes ran trains over the southern portion of its route.

Many of the locomotives and items of rolling stock used on these preserved lines of the standard gauge are owned by private individuals or groups of enthusiasts forming a syndicate, although others are owned by societies such as the '8F' Preservation Society, Great Western Preservations Limited or the Worcester Locomotive Society. They are usually on loan to the group or company in question and this is now the only satisfactory way in which a private person is able to keep a preserved locomotive in good trim and running order. A privately owned steam locomotive may be considered by many to be the ultimate goal of collectors and enthusiasts. Yet apart from the space required and initial cost, even a static locomotive becomes a pile of backyard junk without considerable maintenance and the regular upkeep this involves. Most of the preservation companies either employ skilled professionals or include members and enthusiasts who are also professional railwaymen with experience of driving steam locomotives for British Railways or working in railway repair shops. It is heartening news that Carnforth (Steam Town) and Tyseley (Birmingham), which are both museum depôts, plan to install machinery that may one day assist with heavy repairs and overhauls which all steam locomotives eventually require.

While British Railways were in the process of running down their large stocks of steam locomotives in favour of diesel traction during the mid-1960s it was still possible to buy a main line engine in fair condition for about £1,500. With the majority of steam locomotives now consigned to the breaker's yard or reserved for preservation, the main source of supply seems to have dried up. An alternative is for the would-be private owner to approach an industrial concern which still uses a small fleet of steam shunting engines with a view to acquiring one of these as and when they become redundant. Such locomotives, both steam and diesel, are sometimes offered for sale through the medium of the trade or railway press. It is essential, however, to seek expert advice and valuation, when making a purchase, as locomotives sold at scrap prices may be worth little more than scrap value.

On the subject of industrial and privately owned railways these now offer the enthusiast for the traditional scene even more variety and interest than British Railways. Standardisation, closures and economy drives have tended to reduce the former diverse elements of the main line network to the 'basic railway' favoured by the practical economists now running the system. Fortunately there are still large numbers of factories, mines and dockyards operating either internal systems or exchange sidings which feed into the main lines of British Railways. While some of these, such as the Derwent Valley Railway, hire locomotives and rolling stock from BR the majority still retain their own engines and wagons, many of the former still powered by steam. It is on private lines that such exotic survivals as crane engines, fireless locomotives and coal trucks in private-owner liveries exist many years after disappearing from the public system (plate 10).

The best way in which to view or visit industrial railways is to watch the columns of the railway press devoted to such fixtures and join a rail tour organised by one of the numerous railway or transport societies now flourishing in most parts of the country. These fixtures are usually open to non-members and for a modest fee one is allowed access to the railway with a conducted tour over running sheds and workshops—places normally banned to private individuals.

8. RAILWAY AND TRANSPORT MUSEUMS

There are about twenty transport and railway museums in the British Isles, including an impressive municipal collection at Belfast in Northern Ireland.

These cover all aspects of railway operation from narrow-gauge and industrial systems to main line railways and the early plateways preceding the invention of flanged wheel and edge rails. They provide the railway enthusiast and student of transport history with a unique opportunity to see and examine items which no book or picture may fully describe. At **Derby Museum** there is even a working model railway in which every item of stock and lineside features combine to present a typical cross-section of the former Midland Railway (later absorbed into the London Midland and Scottish Railway) during the period before the First World War (plate 11).

Most of the railway museums of Britain are run by national and municipal bodies each containing large items either loaned or donated by British Railways. The most important of these is the **Museum of British Transport** housed in a former bus garage in the South London district of Clapham. This has been described as the most comprehensive transport museum in Europe, formerly administered by BR but now run by the Ministry of Education and Science. It is unfortunate that since the mid-1960s the future of the museum has been a subject for controversy, with plans for closure and the transfer of more valuable exhibits to an older railway museum at York. This appears to be part of an economy drive and a wish to decentralise, concentrating the main railway exhibits in a provincial centre away from the metropolis. Many who question the wisdom of this move realise that such transfers would be selective and that only the more valuable items would be retained with large numbers of relics offered for sale or consigned to the scrap heap. Outstanding exhibits at Clapham include the record-breaking engine *Mallard,* an ex-LNER streamlined 4-6-2 (Pacific) which still holds the world speed record for steam—now unlikely to be beaten as steam railways gradually disappear from most parts of the world.

Another important centre in the London area for locomotives and relics is the **Science Museum**, Exhibition Road, South Kensington. This has a large number of both full-scale exhibits and working models, with a new gallery of land transport—a considerable portion of which is devoted to railways. Exhibits range from the original *Rocket* of George Stephenson to the original 'Castle Class' 4-6-0 locomotive of the GWR—representing one of the finest and most efficient classes of steam locomotives in the world. There is also the prototype *Deltic* in its original livery—the latter being one of the first of many diesel-electric locomotives to run express services on British Railways.

For many years the **Railway Museum at York** was the only public collection of its kind devoted entirely to railways. York was the headquarters of the North Eastern Railway Company, which eventually controlled the Stockton and Darlington system, thus claiming to be the oldest steam operated railway in the world. Its employees and executives were justly proud of these traditions and many fine relics were preserved at York under the care of Mr. J. B. Harper, an Assistant Superintendent of the line and an enthusiast in his own right. After the grouping the old North Eastern became part of the LNER and many of the relics were consigned to semi-retirement in backyard and basement, not available to the general public. Yet during the Stockton and Darlington Centenary Celebrations in 1925 some of them were brought to light for display purposes and received an enthusiastic reception as part of our national heritage. It was decided that such items should be available for study and general interest in a national railway museum sited at either Darlington or York. York was the final choice, being the headquarters of the former NE Company and more accessible to the general public. By way of compensation two early locomotives were sent to Darlington for permanent exhibition at the Bank Top Station, one of these being *Locomotion No. 1*. built by George Stephenson for the opening of the S and D in 1825. The present museum collection at York, with its accent on the northern half of the country, is supplemented by locomotives and relics from all regions. Most of the larger items are displayed in the repair shops of the original motive power department.

Perhaps the most famous locomotive preserved at York is the 4-2-2 express passenger engine designed by Patrick Stirling, once described as the most attractive design—from an artistic viewpoint—yet produced. It is renowned for taking part in the great railway race to the north, representing the Great Northern Railway on the East Coast route, as locomotive No. 1 in their stud book. Another famous Great

Northern locomotive exhibited at York Museum, also renowned for its charm of design, is No. 990 *Henry Oakley,* the first 4-4-2 'Atlantic' type locomotive built in this country, designed and constructed at Doncaster Works in 1898. York was also the first home in retirement of the GWR 4-4-0 locomotive *City of Truro,* which is claimed to have been the first British steam locomotive to have run at more than 100 m.p.h. in actual service. During the 1950s it was withdrawn from the museum and refurbished to run at the head of a number of special trains, also taking part in a publicity scheme for television services in the West of England. It frequently ran with the former 4-4-0 Midland Compound No. 1000, now preserved at Clapham. By popular request *City of Truro* was not returned to York but presented to the newly opened Great Western Railway Museum at Swindon, a town which may be termed the home of the former GWR.

The exhibits at **Swindon Museum** are housed in a former non-conformist chapel from which the box pews and galleries have been removed. It contains several locomotives, early signalling equipment, scale models—including the first authentic scale model of an actual locomotive ever produced—and relics of the smaller railways, both standard and narrow-gauge, absorbed by the GWR at and before the grouping. There are also personal relics of Brunel, the first engineer and creator of the GWR, displayed in a special 'Brunel Room'. Although an excellent collection of its kind, it suffers from lack of space and room for expansion.

The present **Railway Museum at Leicester**, opened in 1968, contains many relics of the old Midland Railway including the famous Johnson 'Spinner' (4-2-2) No. 118, and an early electric locomotive of the North Eastern Railway dating back to 1904. It is understood that the present restricted quarters of the museum—a former tram depôt—are only temporary and that the exhibits will eventually move to a site in Abbey Lane, now occupied by a large pumping station. This will make it possible to exhibit engines and relics of the Great Central Railway and the ex-LNER 'V2' locomotive *Green Arrow.* The collection will then be termed Leicester Museum of Transport and Technology.

The main collection of locomotives and equipment connected with industrial, quarry and mineral railways is the **Locomotive Museum at Penrhyn Castle,** now administered by the National Trust (plate 12). This is renowned for its wide range of tank locomotives and relics from the slate quarries of North Wales and various factory sites in all parts of Britain. There is also an interesting working model of the former Penrhyn Quarry Railway, constructed by pupils and staff of a local secondary school. This occupies the total length of the stable block at the main entrance to the museum and has a fascinating harbour section with mixed-gauge sidings. It is hoped that a passenger-carrying miniature railway may soon run, in connection with the museum, powered by the only accurate (working) scale model of a compound steam locomotive in existence. This is now undergoing a complete rebuild and overhaul in the hands of the chief engineer. Part of the museum also contains a vintage collection of Bassett-Lowke model railway equipment in the larger gauges, which should prove of interest to the model railway enthusiast and train collector. This originally formed part of an outdoor layout at the Cotswold manor of Snowshill, also belonging to the National Trust.

The previously mentioned narrow-gauge museum at **Towyn Wharf** is adjacent to the terminus of the Talyllyn Railway, and may be visited either before or after a trip on the line. It contains numerous locomotives, items of rolling stock, models and other small exhibits, plus a vintage narrow-gauge locomotive of French origin. Most of the exhibits are from the mines and quarries of Wales. One of the locomotives, an 0-4-0 steam engine formerly operated by the London Brick Company, is now on loan to the Welshpool and Llanfair Light Railway.

It is also important to mention the working and static displays exhibited at **Bressingham Hall**, near Diss, Norfolk, one of the main centres for railway preservation in the eastern counties. This is a private museum connected with an operational narrow-gauge passenger line and several miniature railways of different gauges. One of the main exhibits in the standard-gauge section is the BR 'Britannia' class locomotive (4-6-2) *Oliver Cromwell,* loaned to the museum by British Railways and frequently operated over a short length of track in the grounds of the hall.

Interesting items connected with railways are on display to the public at Bristol Museum, Birmingham Museum of Science and Industry, Swansea Industrial Museum, The Science and Engineering Museum at Newcastle-on-Tyne, Norwich Museum and Staffordshire County Museum at Shugborough Hall near Stafford.

North of the border the Royal Scottish Museum, Edinburgh, has numerous items of interest to the transport historian. The Museum of Transport at Glasgow is one of the finest collections in Britain, especially for relics of the former Scottish main line companies.

The **Pendon Museum**, near Abingdon, Berkshire, is also worthy of note, especially for railway enthusiasts with a leaning towards the GWR and railways of the south-west. It contains working model layouts based on GWR practice in different parts of the West Country, with the intention not only of recording a railway system but also the type of country through which it ran before the days of intensive farming, motorways and council estates. Both railway and lineside features have been reproduced with almost breath-taking accuracy, including one of the famous wooden viaducts designed by Brunel, once an important feature of all railways west of the Tamar. It is claimed that certain lineside cottages are thatched with human hair and that one contains a miniature portrait of an English king in naval uniform showing the orders and medals on his tunic no larger than pinheads.

Before closing this section it may be thought relevant to mention the excellent tramways museum at **Crich**, Derbyshire. Most railway enthusiasts are also interested in tramways, both for their own sake and their close connection with railways. This is in every sense a working museum with examples of electric, steam, cable and horse trams from all parts of the world, although the majority are representative of street tramways operating in leading towns and cities of Britain between the 1860s and 1950s. These vehicles are run over a former quarry line built on the site of an even earlier railway engineered by George Stephenson and opened in 1841. Of special interest to railway enthusiasts is the steam tram engine, the first of its kind, constructed in 1885 to a design patented by William Wilkinson. It was built by Messrs. Beyer, Peacock of Gorton, Manchester, for service in Australia, but was found to be heavy on fuel and returned to the works in England for modifications. Although an essentially experimental type it was not returned to main line duties and worked for nearly fifty years as a yard shunter in the Gorton foundries of Beyer, Peacock. A further industrial-type locomotive preserved at Crich is the English Electric engine *Franklin,* of a class produced mainly for work in the yards and sidings of electricity power stations. It was originally owned by Blackpool Corporation Tramways, both shunting and handling coal traffic in standard mineral wagons, between a junction with the LMS Railway and a depôt of the Fleetwood Tramways system. It was later used to haul works trains, for the permanent-way and engineering departments, when coal traffic ceased in 1949. It is distinguished by a central steeple cab of a type more frequently associated with European and North American systems than the electric railways of Britain.

9. PHOTOGRAPHY AND SKETCHING

Photographing and sketching railways are branches of the hobby which seem to have greatly increased in popularity during the past few years. This is understandable enough as anyone with a scrap of talent or enthusiasm may be only too eager to record their experience and revive agreeable memories. Since the Second World War, standards of photography in particular have improved beyond all recognition, which may reflect a more serious yet less inhibited approach on the part of 'mere amateurs'. While railway and industrial subjects have been liberated from the range of third class subject matter, once barely acceptable in aesthetic circles, this may also have had a liberating effect on painter and photographer.

While photography has its acknowledged creative and experimental side it is certain that where great accuracy is needed this is the medium to be preferred. With most railway subjects—from the painter's viewpoint—especially those involving locomotives and trains, it is often a race against time to make a worthwhile impression before a change of signals. Snags encountered in photography may include the unwanted puff of steam or haze of diesel smoke, the flurry of rain or snow—all of which may obscure working parts and impose a limit on factual interests. It may be seen, in this respect, that despite his spontaneity the photographer is even more at the mercy of bad weather and the unexpected than his counterpart with the brushes.

Articles in almost any magazine on either amateur sketching or photography may offer advice on correct angles, dramatic use of lighting and hints on the best technical use of new equipment. These have an important rôle to play in acquiring basic skills although perhaps the best advice for the amateur is to keep practicing and acquire a wide range of experience.

Try not to exhibit or even seek a market too early. This fairly obvious mistake occurs all too frequently, leading to searing criticism, lack of faith and eventual discouragement. Try to see as many examples of the work of other people—in as wide a technical range as possible. Visit exhibitions of photography, paintings and prints, and make a serious attempt to exploit new angles and views, both in subject matter and composition. Too much creative effort has been wasted on the photography of 'front ends', famous expresses and important main lines. There is a whole range of unexpected and untapped material in station architecture from the wayside halt to the city terminus. The pattern of rails, points and crossings, seen from the angle of an over bridge, high fence or embankment frequently makes a challenging subject, even without traffic. Scenes on industrial lines, narrow-gauge systems or in running shed and railway workshop may offer far more, to both painter and photographer, than the same old three-quarter view of the London express dashing through a familiar diagonal on the horizontal plane.

Many of the older and traditional railway stations—in both town and country—are worth recording for their own sake and as vital evidence in time of threatened destruction. This also applies to goods sheds, tunnel mouths, signal-boxes and a wide range of other similar constructions. It does not mean, however, that modern railway architecture should be ignored or neglected. The railways are among the few locations in modern Britain where old and not so old buildings are being demolished but at least replaced by works of character relating to their setting. Having visited a well-known city in the Midlands to view the modern cathedral, shopping centre and other delights of town planning, the author was more than relieved to return to the modern railway station, which seemed a great improvement on more widely publicised amenities. Fine buildings and excellent pictorial material are often found in unexpected places so do not give up the search too soon. While not wishing to detract from the main buildings of New Street station, Birmingham, the new power signal-box at the northern end of the station is impressive enough to make its surroundings appear mundane.

Whatever your views on subject matter or merits and defects of the foreground, always remember to make the best possible use of skyscape and weather conditions. The piled clouds and odd shaft of sunlight, even gusty winds and effects of rain showers are useful stage properties to exploit with feeling and imagination. Weather to be dreaded from certain viewpoints may be seen as much an ally as an enemy—granted a fair amount of luck—while dodging wind and rain is one of the occupational risks of off-shore Western Europe. The waterproof raincoat, both to wear and as a protective wrapping or groundsheet, is often a great boon to the artist in any medium, while the ample pocket space of these garments is ideal for small equipment.

Make sure that wherever you go in search of a picture you have full permission to intrude. Seeking help and co-operation from railway staff is not only good manners and the correct legal approach but prevents ill-feeling between amateur and professional. While there may be no need to arrive on location groomed for a fashion plate, it is the ill-mannered, awkward person who tends to be misunderstood—drawing suspicion on both himself and his friends. While admiring the grit of the so-called 'gricers' of the sixties, young men who devoted their whole leisure time to photographing the last of particular classes and types of steam engines, it is certain that a rabble of unkempt youths in soiled jeans leaping and crouching on both sidings and running lines made an unfortunate impression on railway workers and officials alike. Such memories take a great deal of living down so that thoughtless conduct reacts not only on the culprits but makes things harder for those who come later or wish to return. Wherever possible write a letter or make a personal contact well in advance of the intended visit.

There is a widely held opinion that installations controlled by preservation groups are open to all and sundry. This is far from true as, except on visiting days or when permission has been granted by someone in charge, it is just as much a trespass to wander about a preserved branch line as to enter the goods yards or running sheds of British Railways. In this connection it should be remembered that rules are made not only to exclude unwanted and irresponsible elements but to avoid fatal accidents. There is an impressive annual list of casualties on even the most efficient railways and because railway travel is often equated with safety in a relaxed atmosphere, this is only true at platform level or in the comfort of a warm compartment. Fortunately there are still plenty of sites both on and near railway property where the artist is able to see all he needs out of harm's way. Unauthorised wandering is never advisable, however safe, quiet and deserted a location seems at the moment of discovery.

10. RAILWAY SLANG AND JARGON

The following is a selection not only of everyday slang used by employees of the modern railways, but describes familiar terms used in most literature and conversations on the railway theme, with reference to the pre-grouping era and early history of the subject.

Austin Seven: Class three Midland goods engine.

Autos: automatic couplings.

Back board: distant signal.

Back shift: working a late turn or shift.

Badge porter: railway porter working outside the main station area; not a platform porter.

Banger: fog signal.

Banjo: fireman's shovel.

Bible: book of rules and regulations.

Birdcage: guard's van having a raised section of glazed roof, through which the guard may observe the line ahead. The term is also applied to a signal-box on a gantry.

Black five: Class five LMR locomotive 4-6-0.

Black prince: locomotive cleaner.

Bloomer: locomotive of the LNWR, a 2-2-2 with 7′ driving wheels.

Blue flash: powerful electric locomotive.

Blue one: green signal aspect.

Board: signal arm.

Bobby: signalman or engineer. These employees were formerly dressed and trained as railway policemen.

Book: working timetable.

Booking on: engine crew reporting for duty, usually an hour before 'booking out'.

Booking out: exact time at which a locomotive leaves the shed for the main line. This is recorded.

Bosh: mixture of boiling water and chemicals used for cleaning the underframes of rolling stock.

Bowling green: fast, clear line ahead.

Brains: an official of traffic control.

Brake stick: rod or pole used by shunters for manipulating hand brakes on rolling stock.

Brown one: distant signal.

Buck jumper: six-coupled tank engine of the GER.

Bug box: old-fashioned four-wheeled passenger carriage.

Bug dust: locomotive coal broken small.

Bunny: pilotman.

Chip bin: lineside ballast box used in repairing a small section of track.

Christmas tree: gantry with numerous colour-light signals

Cinderella's glass coach: inspection saloon used by the District Engineer.

Cockney: name used on GWR and WR for visiting LMS/LMR trains and crew.

Crab: Fowler C4 tender engine 2-6-0 of the MR.

Cracker: fog signal.

Cripple: item of damaged rolling stock.

Cripple road (siding): siding on which damaged rolling stock may be stored, awaiting repairs.

Crow: signal made by the driver on the whistle of a steam engine.

D.C.M.: 'Don't come Monday'. Suspension from normal duties.

Dead engine: steam locomotive with rods uncoupled and fire dropped.

Desert devil: employee responsible for sanding and watering a locomotive ready for the road.

Dinting: clearing out old ballast.

Dogs: pincers used for lifting rails and sleepers.

Doggy: platelayer; man using dogs.

Dolly: small signal posts set on a bracket or gantry; also ground signal used for shunting.

Donkey: small diesel shunting locomotive.

Do it yourself kit: steam locomotive.

Double-heading: two locomotives coupled together to haul a single train.

Double home run: engine crew lodging overnight at a terminus before making the return trip next day.

Down the nick: short of steam.

Down the plug: water in tanks or tender running low.

Down the slot: a slow train running on a fast line.

Drag: sand drag used for stopping runaways on steep bank.

Dummy: ground signal in the form of a disc.

Dwarf: ground signal.

Ell-of-a-Mess: London Midland and Scottish Railway.

Fish and chip car/van: sentinel steam rail car as used on the LNER, mainly in the eastern counties.

Flat: worn part of a wheel caused by skidding.

Fly shunt: illegal method of shunting uncoupled wagons. This is done by the locomotive in charge giving the wagons a sudden push forwards.

Fogging: setting fog signals.

Foreign Legion: men on loan from a different company or region.

Fresher: buffet or refreshment room.
Frothblower: Fowler Class five 2-6-0 tender engine.
Gate box: building to house mechanism for opening level-crossing gates. Not a block post.
Gobbler: steam locomotive greedy for coal. Name given to certain 2-4-2 tank engines of the GER.
Go When Ready: Great Western Railway.
God's Wonderful Railway: Great Western Railway.
Guard's bedroom: brake van on a slow goods train.
Gunboat: tank locomotive on the SER, 144 class, 0-4-4.
Hard up: short of steam.
Hole, The: term used on GW and WR for the Severn Tunnel.
Hooker: shunter.
Horse and cart: slow goods train.
Hot box: axle box overheated through lack of lubricants or overwork.
Hot pot: emission of steam from safety valves.
Hump yard: goods yards or sidings worked by gravity shunting methods.
Hunting: sideways movement or oscillation of bogies, usually on a long run of straight, level track; frequently a running fault with 4-4-0 locomotives.
In steam: Ready to go; a locomotive with steam up.
Iron lung: long-boilered engine; ex-WD 2-8-0 goods locomotive.
Island: island platform with running lines on both sides. Passengers may approach by means of a subway or over bridge.
Jacko: slang term used on WR for a small shunting locomotive.
Jack trap: spring-operated catch points to stop a backward runaway on a steep bank.
Jazz trains: suburban coaching stock of the 1930s with coloured stripes on doors to denote class.
Jersey Lilies: 'Atlantic' locomotives of the GCR. Elegant and sophisticated, named after the society beauty Lily Langtry, also known as 'the Jersey Lily'.
Jim Crow: permanent-way tool used for bending or straightening a length of rail.
Jinties: Class three 0-6-0 tank engines of the LMS.
Jock: packed meal.
Jock tin: food container.
Jumbo: heavy locomotive of the Midland Railway.
Jumbos: locomotives of the LNWR 'Precedent' Class (used for heavy duties), 2-4-0 with 6' 9" driving wheels.

Jumper: ticket collector travelling on a passenger train.

Killer: diesel train, so named on account of its swift yet silent approach.

Kings: locomotive drivers on the Southern Region.

Knobber up: shunter operating points in a goods yard.

Knotty: North Staffordshire Railway Company. So named after the Staffordshire Knot used on its crest and seal, and rolling stock.

Languisher and Yawner: Lancashire and Yorkshire Railway Company.

Lanky: an employee of the Lancashire and Yorkshire Railway Company.

Late and Never Early: London and North Eastern Railway.

Let Me Sleep: London Midland and Scottish Railway.

Link duty: periods of duty for train crews.

Links: four men or two crews working four duties, day and night, in rotation.

Live engine: engine in steam but not ready to go.

Lizzies: 'Pacific' locomotives of the LMS.

Lollipop: shafted wooden tool used for testing sleepers.

Long drag: up hill run from Carlisle to Settle on MR.

Making up: marshalling a train.

Metals: running rails.

Mike: slang term for a shunting engine used on the ER.

Money box: Royal Mail train or coach.

Monkey tail: handle used to open the door of a goods wagon or van.

Motions: gear and rodding causing the valves to operate on a locomotive for the distribution of steam.

Motorman: driver of an electric train.

Mountains of the moon: ash heap in a locomotive yard.

Mowing machines: ungainly type of locking frames used in mechanical signal-boxes of the GNR.

Mud, Sludge and Lightning: Manchester, Sheffield and Lincolnshire Railway.

Muddle and Go Nowhere: Midland and Great Northern Railway.

Nag: diesel shunting engine of 350 h.p.

Noddy: diesel shunting engine of 100 h.p.

Notching up: saving steam on a moving engine by notching the reversing handle in such a way as to restrain the movement of certain valves.

Number snatcher: checker of goods wagons and rolling stock.

Number taker: employee checking vehicles entering or leaving a goods yard.

Old, Worse and Worser: Oxford, Worcester and Wolverhampton Railway. Later absorbed by GWR.
On the floor: derailed goods wagon or carriage.
On the juice: running over the lines of an electric railway.
On the handle: driving an electric or diesel train.
On the shovel: driving a steam engine.
Overlanded: freight arriving late but without record or invoice.
Packer: ballast packer or platelayer.
Paddy: train conveying coal from the pithead to distant sidings.
Pathway: clear route.
Peg: signal.
Pick up goods: slow freight train, picking up and dropping wagons at various wayside stations.
Pick up post: post to which staff or token is attached for single-line workings.
Pilotman: driver taking charge of single-line workings, especially when one line of a double track is under repair.
Pimple: gravity shunting hump in a goods yard.
Porridge: sludge or mud.
Porridge box/pot: The *Royal Scot* express train of LMS running from Euston to Glasgow.
Prince of Wales: short for Prince of Wales' feathers, a plume-like emission of steam.
Pug: saddle tank engine of L & Y 0-4-0 used as a yard and dock shunter.
Pullman: WR term for a shunter's truck.
Pull the string: release of vacuum brakes.
Put away: parking a set or rake of coaches on a siding, after duty.
Put inside: running a less important train or engine into a siding to make way for an express.
Quarter fare: free ticket, privilege fare.
Queen Mary: large goods brake van of a type formerly used on SR.
'Q' train: special train not shown on public timetables.
Raft: goods wagons or vans running together while shunting is carried out; not part of a regular train.
Rake: a number of carriages marshalled together in one train.
Razor gang: economy experts from headquarters.
Red devil: standard Midland Compound locomotive of MR and LMS 4-4-0.
Ride the cushions: train crew returning from duty in a passenger compartment.

Ringer: crowbar used in platelaying.
R.O.: open wagon.
Roundhouse: engine shed with central turntable.
Runner: platform inspector.
Runners: shunters in a goods yard running alongside a moving goods wagon to apply the hand brakes.
Running repairs: small scale repairs carried out in a 'running' or engine shed.
Running shed: engine shed.
Saddlebacks: saddle tank locomotives of the '330' class of the LSWR.
Set back: shunting movement towards rather than away from the shunter.
Setting down: detraining passengers.
Sewer rat: driver or motorman on the underground railways.
Shark: ticket inspector.
Sick and tired: signals and telecommunications.
Silent death: electric train—moving silently but at speed.
Six foot: space of 6′ 5½″ between the running tracks.
Sleeper: second man on a diesel locomotive.
Slow and Dirty: Somerset and Dorset Railway.
Slow Easy and Comfortable: South Eastern and Chatham Railway.
Smudger: engine cleaner.
Snap: packed lunch.
Snap tin: lunch box.
Snip: ticket collector at a station.
Spam can: streamlined locomotive of the SR.
Sparkler: electric train.
Spiv day: easy day or day of rest.
Sprag: goods guard on the ER.
Spluder: the indirect cause of trouble. WR slang.
Square wheels: anything in a run down condition; wheels worn down by overwork.
Stale: overdue goods traffic.
Stinker: wagon delayed for an extra day or two in a goods yard or private siding.
Stripping: removing old ballast and sleepers before repairing track.
S.W. board: 'Sound Whistle' board; a trackside board as used on WR.
Sweat box: heavy jack used in track repairs.
Swedy: the Great Eastern Railway, which served a rural and mainly farming area noted for corn and root crops.
Swinger: an additional coach or van at the end of a train.

Switching out: closing a signal-box or block post by pre-arrangement.

Table: running surface of a rail.

Tapper: carriage and wagon examiner employed in tapping wheels for soundness of metal.

Ticket snapper: ticket collector.

Toffee apple: cake or ball of pitch.

Trail boss: station master or station manager.

Train path: vacant line in the timetable which may be used by an extra train.

Treacle toffee: Welsh steam coal.

Tunnel motor: pannier tank engine of GWR origin, fitted with special condensing apparatus for work over certain lines of the underground railways.

Turn outs: points.

Turn plate: wagon turntable.

Ukelele: 'J39' class locomotive of the LNER.

Under the arm: not up to previous standards.

Under the hammer: signalman's slang for 'train accepted with due caution'.

Up the madhouse: SR term for working a train into a London terminus.

Wagon sheet: tarpaulin.

Walking the length: a ganger making his round of inspection.

Water boiler: fireman on a steam locomotive.

Wells Fargo: early type of Pullman carriage used with steam locomotives.

Wessey: employee of the LNWR.

Womming: term used on the GWR and GCR for rail turning.

Z iron: door stop on a goods wagon.

Zero post: commencement of a main line from which miles are numbered.

Zone fare: flat rate of passenger fares, in a prescribed area.

Zoo box: mess van or carriage.

'Hunt' Class Nameplate

11. RAILWAY PERIODICALS AND SOCIETIES

Periodicals

Model Railway Constructor Monthly. Ian Allan, Terminal House, Shepperton, Middlesex.

Model Railways Monthly. Model and Allied Publications Ltd., 13-35 Bridge St., Hemel Hempstead, Herts.

Modern Railways Monthly. Ian Allan.

Modern Tramways and Light Railways Review Monthly. Ian Allan.

Railway Gazette Fortnightly. Transport and Technical Publications, 161-166 Fleet St., London EC4.

Railway Magazine Monthly. 161-166 Fleet St., London EC4.

Railway Modeller Monthly. Peco Publications and Publicity, Pecoway, Seaton, Devon.

Railway World Monthly. Ian Allan.

Trains Illustrated Quarterly. Ian Allan.

Societies

A list of some of the leading societies mainly concerned with general railway or model railway interests.

Historical Model Railway Society
HQ address: L. Mole, 35 Strode Road, Forest Gate, E7.

Locomotive Club of Great Britain
HQ address: J. M. Cramp, 8 Lovatt Close, Edgware, Mx.

Model Railway Club
HQ address: Keen House, 4 Calshot Street, London N1.

Newcomen Society (The)
The Science Museum, Exhibition Road, London SW7.

Railway and Canal Historical Society
J. R. Harding, 38 Station Road, Wylde Green, Sutton Coldfield, Warks.

The Railway Club
HQ address: 112, High Holborn, London WC1.

Railway Correspondence and Travel Society
HQ address: 82 Natal Road, New Southgate, London N11.

Railway Society of Scotland
HQ address: W. A. Bishop, 21 Corstorphine Bank Drive, Edinburgh 12.

Signalling Record Society (The)
Secretary/Treasurer: J. Morris Esq., Lloyds Bank House, Whitland, Carmarthenshire.

Stephenson Locomotive Society
HQ address: G. K. H. Kerley, 34 Durley Avenue, Pinner, Mx.

Transport Ticket Society (The)
HQ address: J. E. Shelbourn, 18 Villa Road, Luton, Beds.

12. ABBREVIATIONS

Abbreviations for various pre-grouping and pre-nationalised railway companies of Great Britain and Ireland.

BCDR	Belfast and County Down Railway
CBSCR	Cork, Bandon and South Coast Railway
CR	Caledonian Railway
DSER	Dublin and South Eastern Railway
FR	Furness Railway
GCR	Great Central Railway
GER	Great Eastern Railway
GNR	Great Northern Railway
GNR (I)	Great Northern Railway of Ireland
GNSR	Great North of Scotland Railway
GSWR	Glasgow and South Western Railway
GSWR (I)	Great South Western Railway (of Ireland)
GWR	Great Western Railway
HBR	Hull and Barnsley Railway
HR	Highland Railway
IWCR	Isle of Wight Railway
LBSCR	London, Brighton and South Coast Railway
LCDR	London, Chatham and Dover Railway
LMSR	London, Midland and Scottish Railway
LNER	London and North Eastern Railway
LNWR	London and North Western Railway
LSWR	London and South Western Railway
LYR	Lancashire and Yorkshire Railway
MCR	Maryport and Carlisle Railway
MGNJR	Midland and Great Northern Joint Railway
MGWR (I)	Midland and Great Western Railway (of Ireland)
NBR	North British Railway
NER	North Eastern Railway
NLR	North London Railway
NSR	North Staffordshire Railway
PWJR	Portpatrick and Wigtownshire Joint Railway
SDJR	Somerset and Dorset Joint Railway
SECR	South Eastern and Chatham Railway
SER	South Eastern Railway
SR	Southern Railway
TVR	Taff Vale Railway

INDEX

Titles in paperback in the 'Discovering' series:

Printed by C. I. Thomas & Sons (Haverfordwest) Ltd., Press Buildings, Merlin's Bridge, Haverfordwest, Pembrokeshire.